THE ULTRA SIMPLE
Groom's
WEDDING PLANNING GUIDE

From America's Top Wedding Experts,
Elizabeth & Alex Lluch

Authors of Over 3 Million Books Sold!

WS Publishing Group
San Diego, California

THE ULTRA SIMPLE BRIDE AND GROOM WEDDING PLANNING GUIDE

Elizabeth & Alex Lluch
America's Top Wedding Experts and
Authors of Over 3 Million Books Sold

Published by **WS Publishing Group**
San Diego, California 92119
Copyright © 2011 by **WS Publishing Group**

Cover photos: Karen French
www.karenfrenchphotography.com

For inquiries:
Log on to: www.WSPublishingGroup.com
E-mail: info@WSPublishingGroup.com

Printed in China

ISBN: 978-1-936061-23-5

CONTENTS

INTRODUCTION 5

WEDDING PLANNING CHECKLIST 7

BUDGET ANALYSIS 17

ALL ABOUT DIAMONDS 33

GUEST LIST. 43

ADDRESSING INVITATIONS 47

GROOM'S FORMAL WEAR 53

PHOTOGRAPHY 57

CEREMONY OFFICIANT. 65

UNIQUE CEREMONY IDEAS. 67

GIFT REGISTRY 71

RECEPTION. 73

RECEPTION MUSIC. 83

BAKERY 87

CONTENTS

FLOWERS 89

TRANSPORTATION 93

GIFTS 97

PARTIES 99

LEGAL MATTERS 105

TOASTS 107

DO'S AND DON'TS 109

WEDDING PARTY RESPONSIBILITIES 115

TIMELINES 119

WHO PAYS FOR WHAT 131

WEDDING FORMATIONS 133

HONEYMOON 139

INTRODUCTION

Congratulations on your engagement! You must be very excited to have found that special woman to share the rest of your life with. And you must be looking forward to what will be the happiest day of your life — your wedding! Planning a wedding can be fun and exciting. But it can also be very stressful.

Now, more than ever before, grooms are getting involved in wedding planning — lending a hand and voicing their opinions about what kind of wedding they would like to have.

The Ultra Simple Groom's Wedding Planning Guide starts with a detailed checklist of things to do. This list contains everything that a groom is either responsible for or should help his fiancée with. Discuss this list with your fiancée and decide who is going to do what. Remember, planning your wedding should be a joint effort.

The book continues with descriptions of all aspects of the wedding that the groom is traditionally responsible for.

This book also includes a honeymoon planning section to assist you and your bride in making your honeymoon as memorable and enjoyable as it can be.

We are confident that you will find planning your wedding fun and stress-free with the help of *The Ultra Simple Bride and Groom Wedding Planning Guide.*

If you have any comments about this book or suggestions for future editions, please write to us at: Wedding Solutions; 7290 Navajo Road, Suite 207; San Diego, CA, 92119. We listen to grooms like you — that is why *The Ultra Simple Bride and Groom Wedding Planning Guide* is an indispensable wedding guide for the groom!

Sincerely,

Elizabeth H. Lluch

WEDDING PLANNING CHECKLIST

The following Wedding Planning Checklist itemizes everything you need to do or consider when planning your wedding, and gives the best timeframe in which to accomplish each activity.

This checklist assumes that you have nine months or more to plan your wedding. If your wedding is in less than nine months, just start at the beginning of the list and try to catch up as quickly as you can!

Use the boxes to the left of the items to check off activities as you accomplish them. This will enable you to see your progress and help you determine what has been done and what still needs to be done.

NINE MONTHS AND EARLIER

- ❑ Announce your engagement.

- ❑ Select a date for your wedding.

- ❑ Hire a professional wedding consultant.

- ❑ Determine the type of wedding you want:
  location, formality, time of day, number of guests.

- ❑ Determine budget and how expenses will be shared.

- ❑ Develop a record-keeping system for payments made.

- ❑ Consolidate all guest lists: bride's, groom's,
  bride's family, groom's family, and organize:
  1) those who must be invited
  2) those who should be invited
  3) those who would be nice to invite

- ❑ Decide if you want to include children
  among guests.

- ❑ Select and reserve ceremony site.

- ❑ Select and reserve your officiant.

- ❑ Select and reserve reception site.

- ❑ Determine color scheme.

- ❑ Select and book photographer.

- ❑ If ceremony or reception is at home, arrange for
  home or garden improvements as needed.

NINE MONTHS AND EARLIER (CONT.)

❏ Use a calendar to note all important activities: showers, luncheons, parties, get-togethers, etc.

❏ Order passport, visa, or birth certificate, if needed, for your honeymoon or marriage license.

❏ Select maid of honor, best man, bridesmaids, and ushers (approximately one usher per 50 guests).

SIX TO NINE MONTHS BEFORE WEDDING

❏ Select flower girl and ring bearer.

❏ Give *Wedding Party Responsibility Cards* to your wedding party.

❏ Reserve wedding night bridal suite.

❏ Select and book caterer, if needed.

❏ Select and book ceremony musicians.

❏ Select and book reception musicians or DJ.

❏ Schedule fittings and delivery dates for yourself, attendants, and flower girl.

❏ Select and book videographer.

❏ Select and book florist.

❏ Have engagement photos taken.

FOUR TO SIX MONTHS BEFORE WEDDING

❑ Start shopping for each other's wedding gifts.

❑ Reserve rental items needed for ceremony.

❑ Finalize guest list.

❑ Select and order wedding invitations, announcements, and other stationery such as thank-you notes, wedding programs, and seating cards.

❑ Address invitations or hire a calligrapher.

❑ Set date, time, and location for your rehearsal dinner.

❑ Arrange accommodations for out-of-town guests.

❑ Start planning your honeymoon.

❑ Select and book all miscellaneous services, i.e., gift attendant, valet parking, etc.

❑ Register for gifts.

❑ Purchase shoes and accessories.

❑ Begin to break in your shoes.

TWO TO FOUR MONTHS BEFORE WEDDING

❑ Select bakery and order wedding cake.

❑ Order party favors.

❑ Select and order room decorations.

❑ Purchase honeymoon attire and luggage.

TWO TO FOUR MONTHS BEFORE WEDDING (CONT.)

❑ Select and book transportation for wedding day.

❑ Check blood test and marriage license requirements.

❑ Shop for wedding rings and have them engraved.

❑ Consider having your teeth cleaned or bleached.

❑ Consider writing a will and/or prenuptial agreement.

❑ Plan activities for out-of-town guests both before and after the wedding.

❑ Purchase gifts for wedding attendants.

SIX TO EIGHT WEEKS BEFORE WEDDING

❑ Mail invitations. Include accommodation choices and a map to assist guests in finding the ceremony and reception sites.

❑ Maintain a record of RSVPs and all gifts received. Send thank-you notes upon receipt of gifts.

❑ Finalize shopping for wedding day accessories such as toasting glasses, ring pillow, guest book, etc.

❑ Set up an area or a table in your home to display gifts as you receive them.

SIX TO EIGHT WEEKS BEFORE WEDDING (CONT.)

❑ Check with your local newspapers for wedding announcement requirements.

❑ Have the bride's bridal portrait taken.

❑ Check requirements to change the bride's name and address on your driver's license, social security card, insurance policies, subscriptions, bank accounts, etc.

❑ Select and reserve wedding attire for groom, ushers, ring bearer, and father of the bride.

❑ Select a guest book attendant. Decide where and when to have guests sign in.

❑ Mail invitations to rehearsal dinner.

❑ Get blood test and health certificate.

❑ Obtain marriage license.

❑ Look into booking wedding day transportation.

❑ Find "something old, something new, something borrowed, something blue, and a sixpence (or shiny penny) for your shoe."

❑ Finalize your menu, beverage, and alcohol order.

TWO TO SIX WEEKS BEFORE WEDDING

❑ Confirm ceremony details with your officiant.

❑ Arrange final fitting of bridesmaids' dresses.

❑ Have final fitting of bride's gown and headpiece.

❑ Make final floral selections.

❑ Finalize rehearsal dinner plans; arrange seating
and write names on place cards, if desired.

❑ Make a detailed timeline for your wedding party.

❑ Make a detailed timeline for your service providers.

❑ Confirm details with all service providers, including
attire. Give them copies of your wedding timeline.

❑ Start packing for your honeymoon.

❑ Finalize addressing and stamping announcements.

❑ Decide if you want to form a receiving line. If so,
determine when and where to form the line.

❑ Contact guests who haven't responded.

❑ Pick up rings and check for fit.

❑ Meet with photographer and confirm special photos
you want taken.

❑ Meet with videographer and confirm special events
or people you want recorded.

TWO TO SIX WEEKS BEFORE WEDDING (CONT.)

❏ Meet with musicians and confirm music to be played during special events such as the first dance.

❏ Continue writing thank-you notes as gifts arrive.

❏ Remind bridesmaids and ushers of when and where to pick up their wedding attire.

❏ Determine ceremony seating for special guests. Give a list to the ushers.

❏ Plan reception room layout and seating with your reception site manager or caterer. Write names on place cards for arranged seating.

THE LAST WEEK

❏ Pick up wedding attire and make sure everything fits.

❏ Do final guest count and notify your caterer or reception site manager.

❏ Arrange for someone to drive the getaway car.

❏ Gather everything you will need for the rehearsal and wedding day.

❏ Review the schedule of events and last minute arrangements with your service providers. Give them each a detailed timeline.

THE LAST WEEK (CONT.)

❑ Familiarize yourself with guests' names. It will help during the receiving line and reception.

❑ Confirm all honeymoon reservations and accommodations. Pick up tickets and traveler's checks.

❑ Finish packing your suitcases for the honeymoon.

❑ Notify the post office to hold mail while you are away on your honeymoon.

THE REHEARSAL DAY

❑ Put suitcases in getaway car if leaving for your honeymoon the following day.

❑ Give best man the officiant's fee and any other checks for service providers. Instruct him to deliver these checks the day of the wedding.

❑ Arrange for someone to bring accessories such as flower basket, ring pillow, guest book and pen, toasting glasses, cake cutting knife, and napkins to the ceremony and reception.

❑ Arrange for someone to mail announcements the day after the wedding.

THE REHEARSAL DAY (CONT.)

❑ Arrange for someone to return rental items such as tuxedos, slip, and cake pillars after the wedding.

❑ Provide each member of your wedding party with a detailed schedule of events/timelines.

❑ Review ceremony seating with ushers.

THE WEDDING DAY

❑ Give the groom's ring to the maid of honor.

❑ Simply follow your detailed schedule of events.

❑ Relax and enjoy your wedding!

BUDGET ANALYSIS

This comprehensive Budget Analysis has been designed to provide you with all the expenses that can be incurred in any size wedding, including such hidden costs as taxes, gratuities and other items that can easily add up to thousands of dollars in a wedding. After you have completed this budget worksheet, you will have a clear idea of what your wedding will cost. You can then prioritize and allocate your expenses accordingly.

This budget is divided into fifteen categories:
Ceremony, Wedding Attire, Photography, Videography, Stationery, Reception, Music, Bakery, Flowers, Decorations, Transportation, Rental Items, Gifts, Parties and Miscellaneous.

At the beginning of each category, we have indicated the percentage of the wedding budget that is typically spent in that category, based on national averages.

BUDGET ANALYSIS

To determine the total cost of your wedding, estimate the amount of money you will spend on each item in the budget analysis and write that amount in the "Budget" column after each item. Items printed in italics are traditionally paid for by you or your family.

Add all the "Budget" amounts within each category and write that amount in the "Budget Subtotal" space at the end of each category. Then add all the "Subtotal" figures to come up with your final wedding budget. The "Actual" column is for you to input your actual expenses as you purchase items or hire your service providers. Writing down the actual expenses will help you stay within your budget.

If you find, after adding up all your "Budget Subtotals," that the total amount is more than you'd like to spend, simply decide which items are more important to you and adjust your expenses accordingly.

Items in italics are traditionally paid for by the groom or his family.

CEREMONY

- ❑ Ceremony Site Fee
- ❑ *Officiant's Fee*
- ❑ *Officiant's Gratuity*
- ❑ Guest Book/Pen/Penholder
- ❑ Ring Bearer Pillow
- ❑ Flower Girl Basket

WEDDING ATTIRE

- ❑ Bridal Gown
- ❑ Alterations
- ❑ Headpiece/Veil
- ❑ Gloves
- ❑ Jewelry
- ❑ Garter/Stockings
- ❑ Shoes
- ❑ Hairdresser
- ❑ Makeup Artist
- ❑ Manicure/Pedicure
- ❑ *Groom's Formal Wear*

PHOTOGRAPHY

- ❑ Bride & Groom's Album
- ❑ Engagement Photograph
- ❑ Formal Bridal Portrait
- ❑ Parents' Album
- ❑ Proofs/Previews
- ❑ Digital Files
- ❑ Extra Prints

VIDEOGRAPHY

- ❑ Main Video
- ❑ Titles
- ❑ Extra Hours
- ❑ Photo Montage
- ❑ Extra Copies

STATIONERY

- ❑ Invitations
- ❑ Response Cards
- ❑ Reception Cards
- ❑ Ceremony Cards
- ❑ Pew Cards
- ❑ Seating/Place Cards
- ❑ Rain Cards
- ❑ Maps
- ❑ Ceremony Programs
- ❑ Announcements
- ❑ Thank-You Notes
- ❑ Stamps
- ❑ Calligraphy
- ❑ Napkins/Matchbooks

RECEPTION

- ❑ Reception Site Fee
- ❑ Hors d'Oeuvres
- ❑ Main Meal/Caterer
- ❑ Liquor/Beverages
- ❑ Bartending/Bar Setup Fee
- ❑ Corkage Fee
- ❑ Fee to Pour Coffee
- ❑ Gratuity

RECEPTION (CONT.)

- ❑ Service Providers' Meals
- ❑ Party Favors
- ❑ Disposable Cameras
- ❑ Rose Petals/Rice
- ❑ Gift Attendant
- ❑ Parking Fee/Valet Services

MUSIC

- ❑ Ceremony Music
- ❑ Reception Music

BAKERY

- ❑ Wedding Cake
- ❑ *Groom's Cake*
- ❑ Cake Delivery/Setup Fee
- ❑ Cake-Cutting Fee
- ❑ Cake Top
- ❑ Cake Knife/ Toasting Glasses

FLOWERS

BOUQUETS
- ❏ *Bride*
- ❏ Tossing
- ❏ Maid of Honor
- ❏ Bridesmaid

FLORAL HAIRPIECES
- ❏ Maid of Honor/
  Bridesmaids
- ❏ Flower Girl

CORSAGES
- ❏ *Bride's Going Away*
- ❏ *Family Members*

BOUTONNIERES
- ❏ *Groom*
- ❏ *Ushers/Other*
  Family Members

CEREMONY SITE
- ❏ Main Altar
- ❏ Altar Candelabra
- ❏ Aisle Pews

FLOWERS (CONT.)

RECEPTION SITE
- ❏ Head Table
- ❏ Guest Tables
- ❏ Buffet Table
- ❏ Punch Table
- ❏ Cake Table
- ❏ Cake
- ❏ Cake Knife
- ❏ Toasting Glasses
- ❏ Floral Delivery/Setup
  Fee

DECORATIONS
- ❏ Table Centerpieces
- ❏ Balloons

TRANSPORTATION
- ❏ Transportation

RENTAL ITEMS

- ❑ Bridal Slip
- ❑ Ceremony Accessories
- ❑ Tent/Canopy
- ❑ Dance Floor
- ❑ Tables/Chairs
- ❑ Linen/Tableware
- ❑ Heaters
- ❑ Lanterns
- ❑ Other Rental Items

GIFTS

- ❑ *Bride's Gift*
- ❑ Groom's Gift
- ❑ Bridesmaids' Gifts
- ❑ *Ushers' Gifts*

PARTIES

- ❑ Engagement Party
- ❑ *Bachelor Party*
- ❑ Bachelorette Party
- ❑ Bridal Shower
- ❑ Bridesmaids' Luncheon
- ❑ *Rehearsal Dinner*
- ❑ Day-After Brunch

MISCELLANEOUS

- ❑ Newspaper Announcements
- ❑ *Marriage License*
- ❑ *Prenuptial Agreement*
- ❑ Bridal Gown Preservation
- ❑ Bridal Bouquet Preservation
- ❑ Wedding Consultant
- ❑ Wedding Planning Online
- ❑ Taxes

Items in italics are traditionally paid for by the groom or his family.

WEDDING BUDGET	Budget	Actual
YOUR TOTAL WEDDING BUDGET	$	$
CEREMONY (Typically = 5% of Budget)	$	$
Ceremony Site Fee	$	$
Officiant's Fee	$	$
Officiant's Gratuity	$	$
Guest Book/Pen/Penholder	$	$
Ring Bearer Pillow	$	$
Flower Girl Basket	$	$
SUBTOTAL 1	$	$

WEDDING ATTIRE (Typically = 10% of Budget)	$	$
Bridal Gown	$	$
Alterations	$	$
Headpiece/Veil	$	$
Gloves	$	$
Jewelry	$	$
Garter/Stockings	$	$
Shoes	$	$

WEDDING BUDGET	Budget	Actual
WEDDING ATTIRE (CONT.)		
Hairdresser	$	$
Makeup Artist	$	$
Manicure/Pedicure	$	$
Groom's Formal Wear	$	$
SUBTOTAL 2	$	$

	Budget	Actual
PHOTOGRAPHY (Typically = 9% of Budget)	$	$
Bride & Groom's Album	$	$
Engagement Photograph	$	$
Formal Bridal Portrait	$	$
Parents' Album	$	$
Proofs/Previews	$	$
Digital Files	$	$
Extra Prints	$	$
SUBTOTAL 3	$	$

WEDDING BUDGET	Budget	Actual
VIDEOGRAPHY (Typically = 5% of Budget)	$	$
Main Video	$	$
Titles	$	$
Extra Hours	$	$
Photo Montage	$	$
Extra Copies	$	$
SUBTOTAL 4	$	$

STATIONERY		
STATIONERY (Typically = 4% of Budget)	$	$
Invitations	$	$
Response Cards	$	$
Reception Cards	$	$
Ceremony Cards	$	$
Pew Cards	$	$
Seating/Place Cards	$	$
Rain Cards	$	$
Maps	$	$
Ceremony Programs	$	$
Announcements	$	$

WEDDING BUDGET	Budget	Actual
STATIONERY (CONT.)		
Thank-You Notes	$	$
Stamps	$	$
Calligraphy	$	$
Napkins/Matchbooks	$	$
SUBTOTAL 5	$	$

RECEPTION	Budget	Actual
RECEPTION (Typically = 35% of Budget)	$	$
Reception Site Fee	$	$
Hors d'Oeuvres	$	$
Main Meal/Caterer	$	$
Liquor/Beverages	$	$
Bartending/Bar Setup Fee	$	$
Corkage Fee	$	$
Fee to Pour Coffee	$	$
Service Providers' Meals	$	$
Gratuity	$	$
Party Favors	$	$
Disposable Cameras	$	$

WEDDING BUDGET	Budget	Actual
RECEPTION (CONT.)		
Rose Petals/Rice	$	$
Gift Attendant	$	$
Parking Fee/Valet Services	$	$
SUBTOTAL 6	$	$

	Budget	Actual
MUSIC (Typically = 5% of Budget)	$	$
Ceremony Music	$	$
Reception Music	$	$
SUBTOTAL 7	$	$

	Budget	Actual
BAKERY (Typically = 2% of Budget)	$	$
Wedding Cake	$	$
Groom's Cake	$	$
Cake Delivery/Setup Fee	$	$
Cake-Cutting Fee	$	$
Cake Top	$	$
Cake Knife/Toasting Glasses	$	$
SUBTOTAL 8	$	$

WEDDING BUDGET	Budget	Actual
FLOWERS (Typically = 6% of Budget)	$	$
BOUQUETS	$	$
Bride	$	$
Tossing	$	$
Maid of Honor	$	$
Bridesmaids	$	$
FLORAL HAIRPIECES	$	$
Maid of Honor/Bridesmaids	$	$
Flower Girl	$	$
CORSAGES	$	$
Bride's Going Away	$	$
Family Members	$	$
BOUTONNIERES	$	$
Groom	$	$
Ushers/Other Family Members	$	$
CEREMONY SITE	$	$
Main Altar	$	$
Altar Candelabra	$	$
Aisle Pews	$	$

WEDDING BUDGET	Budget	Actual
FLOWERS (CONT.)		
RECEPTION SITE	$	$
Reception Site	$	$
Head Table	$	$
Guest Tables	$	$
Buffet Table	$	$
Punch Table	$	$
Cake Table	$	$
Cake	$	$
Cake Knife	$	$
Toasting Glasses	$	$
Floral Delivery/Setup Fee	$	$
SUBTOTAL 9	$	$

	Budget	Actual
DECORATIONS (Typically = 3% of Budget)	$	$
Table Centerpieces	$	$
Balloons	$	$
SUBTOTAL 10	$	$

WEDDING BUDGET	Budget	Actual
TRANSPORTATION (Typically = 2% of Budget)	$	$
Transportation	$	$
SUBTOTAL 11	$	$

RENTAL ITEMS (Typically = 3% of Budget)	$	$
Bridal Slip	$	$
Ceremony Accessories	$	$
Tent/Canopy	$	$
Dance Floor	$	$
Tables/Chairs	$	$
Linen/Tableware	$	$
Heaters	$	$
Lanterns	$	$
Other Rental Items	$	$
SUBTOTAL 12	$	$

WEDDING BUDGET	Budget	Actual
GIFTS (Typically = 3% of Budget)	$	$
Bride's Gift	$	$
Groom's Gift	$	$
Bridesmaids' Gifts	$	$
Ushers' Gifts	$	$
SUBTOTAL 13	$	$

PARTIES (Typically = 4% of Budget)	$	$
Engagement Party	$	$
Bridal Shower	$	$
Bachelor Party	$	$
Bachelorette Party	$	$
Bridesmaids' Luncheon	$	$
Rehearsal Dinner	$	$
Day-After Brunch	$	$
SUBTOTAL 14	$	$

WEDDING BUDGET	Budget	Actual
MISCELLANEOUS (Typically = 4% of Budget)	$	$
Newspaper Announcements	$	$
Marriage License	$	$
Prenuptial Agreement	$	$
Bridal Gown Preservation	$	$
Bridal Bouquet Preservation	$	$
Wedding Consultant	$	$
Wedding Planning Online	$	$
Taxes	$	$
SUBTOTAL 15	$	$

GRAND TOTAL (Add "Budget" & "Actual" Subtotals 1-15)	$	$

ALL ABOUT DIAMONDS

Throughout the world, diamonds are used to symbolize love and the unbreakable bond of marriage. Searching for a diamond, however, can be very stressful since there are many factors that can affect your decision, such as shape, size, beauty and cost. The following information will give you the knowledge you need to make that very special purchase.

DIAMOND SHAPES

There are various shapes of diamonds. The most popular is the round cut, known as "brilliant." Close to 75 percent of diamonds sold are round. This is mainly because they tend to sparkle more than the other shapes. Other shapes, such as marquise, oval, emerald, princess (or square), and the pear shape, are known as "fancy."

BEFORE YOU BUY

Before purchasing a diamond, you will need to know your fiancée's taste. If you are planning to surprise her, try to purchase your diamond from a reputable source that offers a money back guarantee or at least allows exchange.

DIAMOND LINGO

Boat: The boat is a piece of paper used to hold the diamond upright (in a V-shape) so one can look at the diamond. This paper is extremely white so it allows you to see the diamond's true color.

Brilliance: Brilliance is the amount of sparkle a diamond possesses.

Chips: Chips are external nicks in the girdle of the diamond.

Clouds: Clouds refer to a cloudy area inside the diamond.

Crown: The crown is the part of the diamond above the girdle.

Culet: The culet is the minute bottom facet of the stone.

Facets: Facets are the planes on a diamond which direct light through the stone.

Feathers: Feathers are used to describe a central crack with little cracks along its side.

Fire: Fire is the intensity of colors created by a diamond.

Girdle: The girdle is the rim or edge of the stone having the largest diameter.

Inclusions: Inclusions are the carbon spots inside a diamond which reflect light, making the spot look black.

Scratch: A scratch is a mark on the face of the diamond. Scratches can usually be polished out.

Pavilion: The pavilion is the part of the diamond below the girdle.

Table: The table is the broad top facet of the diamond.

THE FOUR C'S

The famous four C's are the main characteristics that determine the value of a diamond. They refer to color, cut, clarity and carat.

COLOR

A diamond's color scale ranges from D to Z.

D to F: .... Colorless

G to J: .... Near colorless

K to M: ....Faint yellow

N to R: .... Very light yellow

S to Z: .... Light yellow

Z+: .... Fancy or colored

Keep in mind that the slight color of near colorless diamonds is usually visible only through a magnifying lens and from the underside of the diamond. Therefore, minor shades of color, even in diamonds in the I category, are hard to see in mounted stones.

CUT

Cut is the most important element of a diamond. It is what gives the diamond fire and sparkle. Most women would agree that a smaller diamond with a lot of fire and sparkle is better than a bigger diamond without any flair.

A diamond that is cut too shallow may appear larger than a properly cut diamond of the same size, but it may have less sparkle. On the other hand, a diamond that is cut too deep may appear smaller than a properly cut diamond of the same size, but it may look darker.

Prices can vary as much as 50 percent between a well-cut stone and a poorly-cut stone.

CLARITY

The clarity of the diamond is also very important as it allows you to see the diamond's level of perfection. The more imperfections in a diamond, the less fire or sparkle it has. The fewer imperfections in a diamond, the more light that can pass through it.

Clarity is graded on a scale of Flawless (FL), Internally Flawless (IF), Very Very Slight Inclusion (VVS1 and VVS2), Very Slight Inclusion (VSl and VS2), and Slight Inclusion (SI1-SI3). Clarity is always graded under a jeweler's loupe (10x magnification) and always with an experienced eye.

FLAWS OR INCLUSIONS

All diamonds have one or more inclusions, whether visible or not, but no two diamonds have the same inclusion in the same area. Therefore, flaws or inclusions are often referred to as the "fingerprint" of the diamond.

Flawless (FL): An FL diamond contains no imperfections. These diamonds are extremely rare and therefore very expensive.

Internally flawless (IF): An IF diamond has no internal inclusions and very few minor external inclusions.

Very Very Slight Inclusions (VVS1): A VVS1 diamond has very small inclusions, mainly externally. These inclusions are so small that they are hard to find even with a jeweler's loupe.

Very Very Slight Inclusions (VVS2): A VVS2 diamond has a little larger inclusion than the VVS1 but it is still hard to see under a jeweler's loupe.

Very Slight Inclusions 1 (VS1): A VS1 diamond has small inclusions, usually around the edge of the stone. It is not easy to see these inclusions under a jeweler's loupe.

Very Slight Inclusions 2 (VS2): A VS2 diamond has small

inclusions, usually around the heart of the stone. These inclusions may be a little difficult to see under a jeweler's loupe.

Slight Inclusions 1 (SI1): An SI1 diamond has few inclusions, usually around the edge of the diamond. These inclusions are easy to locate under a jeweler's loupe.

Slight Inclusions 2 (SI2): An SI2 diamond has inclusions, usually around the table of the diamond. These inclusions are very easy to locate under a jeweler's loupe.

Slight Inclusions 3 (SI3): An SI3 diamond has inclusions, usually under the table of the diamond. These inclusions are very easy to locate under a jeweler's loupe.

Inclusions 1 (I1): An I1 diamond has several inclusions inside the diamond that are very easy to locate under a jeweler's loupe and may even be seen with the naked eye.

Inclusions 2 (I2): An I2 diamond has several inclusions, usually in the heart of the stone. These inclusions are easily seen by the naked eye.

Inclusions 3 (I3): An I3 diamond has several inclusions that are very easily seen by the naked eye.

CARAT

Carat is the unit used to measure the weight of a diamond. It is equal to 200 milligrams or 142 carats to the ounce. The cost of a diamond increases exponentially as its size or weight increases. For example, a two-carat diamond costs much more than two one-carat diamonds. This is because bigger diamonds are harder to find.

The price point for a carat is about .85-carat. This means that a .80 carat diamond will cost much less than a .90 carat diamond, but a .90 carat diamond will cost almost the same as a 1 carat diamond. So if you have the choice, buy either a .80 carat diamond or, if you can afford it, a 1 carat diamond to get the most for your money.

To save money, set a small side diamond on each side of the center diamond; this will make the center stone look much bigger. Or buy an oval diamond, which is the least expensive shape. Buy your diamond after Christmas or Valentine's Day to take advantage of sales. Summer is also a good time to buy a diamond since jewelers are usually slow during this time.

Keep in mind that color is not too crucial since it is difficult to discern color differences once the diamond is mounted.

Beware of buying a diamond from a fly-by-night operation. Buy from a reputable jeweler who offers a money-back guarantee or at least gives you the option of trading-in your diamond for another one. And make your purchase subject to verification of GIA certification.

Do not rely on verification by a GIA-certified agent recommended by the jeweler who sold you the diamond. Try to find an independent agent or go directly to the GIA. The GIA is the only independent organization which will tell you the true, unbiased characteristics of your diamond without having an interest in selling you something.

BEFORE YOU BUY

Before you purchase a diamond, make sure you get a detailed appraisal of the diamond in writing. Also get in writing any other policy such as money-back or trade-in as well as whether the purchase is subject to verification of GIA certification.

DIAMOND COMPARISON CHART

Compare diamonds from various sources.

Name of Source:

Color:

Cut:

Clarity:

Carat:

Cost:

Name of Source:

Color:

Cut:

Clarity:

Carat:

Cost:

Name of Source:

Color:

Cut:

Clarity:

Carat:

Cost:

GUEST LIST

Start creating your guest list as soon as possible. Ask your parents and the bride's parents for a list of people they would like to invite. You and your fiancée should make your own lists.

Categorize your initial guest list so it is easy to pare down if need be. Group your guests into three different categories: those who must be invited, those who should be invited, and those who it would be nice to invite. This will help you decide who you definitely want to invite to your wedding.

Determine if you wish to invite children; if so, add their names to your list. All children over the age of 16 should receive their own invitation. If you are not inviting children, you can leave their names off the invitations. Only people listed on the invitations should RSVP to the wedding. You may also want to indicate the total number of seats you have reserved for each family, so they will know that you are planning an adults-only wedding.

Things to Consider: Naturally, not everyone you invite to your wedding will be able to attend. For a traditional (non-destination) wedding, if you invite more than 200 guests, estimate that about 75 percent of your guest list will come. If you are inviting fewer than 200 guests, 80 to 85 percent will RSVP that they will attend. For a destination wedding, expect that 50 to 70 percent of your guest list will attend, depending on whether the wedding is being held in the Continental U.S. or in a foreign country. However, you should always plan for every person on your list to RSVP "Yes," to be on the safe side.

You may also want to create a "B list." The B list are people you would like to invite in the event that guests from the original list are unable to attend. Plan to send B invitations out several weeks before the wedding to give those guests time to RSVP.

When making your final guest list, make sure all addresses are current and that names are spelled correctly.

Tips to Save Money: You may find that you are over-budget and need to trim the guest list. This is a difficult task — perhaps the most difficult one you'll face during wedding planning. Start by eliminating people who have been included on your guest list out of courtesy — this means people who you went to school with or grew up with but don't stay in touch with, friends of your parents you don't know (unless your parents are paying for the wedding), coworkers, and people who you are inviting because they invited you to their weddings. You should never feel obligated to invite anyone.

Allowing everyone on your guest list a "plus one" can get very expensive. Only married friends and family, your attendants, and those in a long-term committed relationship should be told to bring a guest.

Consider making your reception "adults-only"; the cost per plate for children, who eat much less, can be nearly as much as the cost for adults.

NOTES

ADDRESSING INVITATIONS

A big way you can assist your bride is by helping to address wedding invitations. This is an arduous task that she will appreciate your help with! If you are working with a wedding consultant, he or she can also help you address invitations.

We recommend that you start addressing your invitations at least three months before your wedding, and preferably four months if your guest list is above 200.

There are typically two envelopes that need to be addressed for wedding invitations: an inner envelope and an outer envelope. The inner envelope is placed unsealed inside the outer envelope, with the flap away from the person inserting.

Start by confirming the spelling of guests' names and that you have their correct addresses. Then, decide how you want to address the envelopes. If you have nice handwriting and want to address them by hand, that is one option.

Another option is to print labels or feed envelopes through a printer and print the addresses directly on the envelope. Another option, for the RSVP card, is to use a stamp with your return address and stamp the envelopes. You can either order one online or buy a stamp-making kit for about $25 from any office supply store.

The invitation and all enclosures are placed inside the inner envelope facing the back flap. The inner envelope contains the name (or names) of the person (or people) who are invited to the ceremony and/or reception. The address is not included on the inner envelope. The outer envelope contains the name (or names) and address of the person (or people) to whom the inner envelope belongs.

Use the guidelines below to help you properly address both the inner and outer envelopes.

GUIDELINES FOR ADDRESSING INVITATIONS

Husband and Wife (with same surname)
> Inner Envelope
> Mr. and Mrs. Smith
>
> Outer Envelope
> Mr. and Mrs. Thomas Smith
> (use middle name, if known)

Husband and Wife (with different surnames)
Inner Envelope
Ms. Banks and Mr. Smith (wife first)

Outer Envelope
Ms. Anita Banks
Mr. Thomas Smith
(wife's name & title above husband's)

Husband and Wife (wife has professional title)
Inner Envelope
Dr. Smith and Mr. Smith

Outer Envelope
Dr. Anita Smith
Mr. Thomas Smith
(wife's name & title above husband's)

Husband and Wife (with children under 16)
Inner Envelope
Mr. and Mrs. Smith
John, Mary, and Glen (in order of age)

Outer Envelope
Mr. and Mrs. Thomas Smith

Single Woman (regardless of age)
Inner Envelope
Miss/Ms. Smith

Outer Envelope
Miss/Ms. Beverly Smith

Single Woman and Guest
Inner Envelope
Miss/Ms. Smith
Mr. Jones (or "and Guest")

Outer Envelope
Miss/Ms. Beverly Smith

Single Man
Inner Envelope
Mr. Jones (Master for a young boy)

Outer Envelope
Mr. William Jones

Single Man and Guest
Inner Envelope
Mr. Jones
Miss/Ms. Smith (or "and Guest")

Outer Envelope
Mr. William Jones

Unmarried Couple Living Together
Inner Envelope
Mr. Knight and Ms. Orlandi
(names listed alphabetically)

Outer Envelope
Mr. Michael Knight
Ms. Paula Orlandi

Two Sisters (over 16)
Inner Envelope
The Misses Smith

Outer Envelope
The Misses Mary and Jane Smith
(in order of age)

Two Brothers (over 16)
Inner Envelope
The Messrs. Smith

Outer Envelope
The Messrs. John and Glen Smith
(in order of age)

Brothers & Sisters (over 16)
Inner Envelope
Mary, Jane, John & Glen
(name the girls first, in order of age)

Outer Envelope
The Misses Smith
The Messrs. Smith
(name the girls first)

A Brother and Sister (over 16)
Inner Envelope
Jane and John (name the girl first)

Outer Envelope
Miss Jane Smith and Mr. John Smith
(name the girl first)

Widow
Inner Envelope
Mrs. Smith

Outer Envelope
Mrs. William Smith

Divorcee
Inner Envelope
Mrs. Smith

Outer Envelope
Mrs. Jones Smith
(maiden name and former husband's surname)

GROOM'S FORMAL WEAR

You should select your formal wear based on the place, time and formality of your wedding. For a semi-formal or formal wedding, you will need a tuxedo. A tuxedo is the formal jacket worn by men on special or formal occasions. The most popular colors are black, white and gray.

Use the following guidelines to select customary attire for your wedding:

Informal:
Business suit
White dress shirt and tie

Semi-formal Daytime:
Formal suit
White dress shirt
Cummerbund or vest
Four-in-hand or bow tie

Semi-formal Evening:
Formal suit or dinner jacket
Matching trousers
White shirt
Cummerbund or vest
Black bow tie
Cufflinks and studs

Formal Daytime:
Cutaway or stroller jacket
Waistcoat
Striped trousers
White wing-collared shirt
Striped tie
Studs and cufflinks

Very Formal Daytime:
Cutaway coat
Wing-collared shirt
Ascot
Striped trousers
Cufflinks
Gloves

Formal Evening:
Black dinner jacket
Matching trousers
Waistcoat
White tuxedo shirt
Bow tie
Cummerbund or vest
Cufflinks

Very Formal Evening:
Black tailcoat
Matching striped trousers
Bow tie
White wing-collared shirt
Waistcoat
Patent leather shoes
Studs and cufflinks
Gloves

In selecting your formal wear, keep in mind the formality and time of day of your wedding, the bride's gown and colors of the bridesmaids' dresses. Consider darker colors for a fall or winter wedding and lighter colors for a spring or summer wedding. When selecting a place to rent your tuxedo, check the reputation of the shop. Make sure they have a wide variety of makes and styles to choose from.

Reserve tuxedos for yourself and your ushers several weeks before the wedding to ensure a wide selection and to allow enough time for alterations. Plan to pick up the tuxedos a few days before the wedding to allow time for last-minute alterations in case they don't fit properly. Out-of-town men in your wedding party can be sized at any tuxedo shop. They can send their measurements to you or directly to the shop where you are going to rent your tuxedos.

Ask about the store's return policy and be sure you delegate to the appropriate person (usually your best man) the responsibility of returning all tuxedos within the time allotted. Ushers customarily pay for their own tuxedos.

Try to negotiate getting your tuxedo for free or at a discount in exchange for having your father, your fiancée's father and your ushers rent their tuxedos at that shop.

NOTES

PHOTOGRAPHY

Your wedding album will be something you look back on for a lifetime with your bride, so choosing a photographer is an important task. Help your bride by discussing the style of wedding photography you want, interviewing multiple vendors together, creating a shot list, and more.

Comprehensive information on wedding photography can be found in the bride's book.

BRIDE & GROOM'S ALBUM

The bride and groom's photo album contains the most photographs and will be looked at repeatedly over the years. Choosing a photographer who will shoot your wedding in the style you want and deliver the shots you want is an important task. Photography packages come in a very wide range of prices and services.

Options: Photographers will tell you that they're skilled in "photo journalistic," "candid" or "editorial" style photography, so look through their portfolios for the style that stands out to you. Some photographers are known for formal poses, while others specialize in more candid, creative shots. Some can capture both.

The industry standard for wedding photographers is now digital film, which is the easiest to print, retouch, and allows the photographer to get the most shots to choose from. However, some photographers still like to use film, or a combination of digital and film. Film forces the photographer to choose and set up each shot carefully and artfully and produces a timeless, romantic and textured photograph. Decide which look and feel you want for your photos.

You also want to inquire as to whether your desired photographer works alone or with a backup shooter or assistant. Having more than one person shooting the wedding means you will have a wider variety of shots, especially candids and special moments that one person could miss. Many times a second photographer will be included in the price of the package.

Finally, there are a large variety of wedding albums. They vary in size, color, material, construction and price. Traditional-style albums frame each individual photo in a mat on the page. Digitally designed "Montage" albums group the photos in a creatively designed fashion for a more modern look. Find one that you like and will feel proud of showing to your friends and family. Some of the most popular manufacturers of wedding albums are Art Leather, Leather Craftsman, Capri and Renaissance. Different papers are also available to print your photos — pearl and metallic as well as black and white can be chosen. Ask to see samples.

Compare at least three photographers for quality, value, and price. Be aware that novice photographers or those who shoot weddings "on the side" are less expensive, but the quality of their photographs may not be as good as a wedding professional. For many couples on budgets, the photography is the area in which they splurge in order to have the best wedding album possible.

Things to Consider: It is always best to hire a photographer who specializes in weddings. Your photographer should be experienced in wedding procedures and familiar with your ceremony and reception sites. This will allow him or her to anticipate your next move and be in the proper place at the right time to capture all the special moments. However, personal rapport is extremely important. The photographer may be an expert, but if you don't feel comfortable or at ease with him or her, your photography will reflect this. Comfort and compatibility with your photographer can make or break your wedding day and your photographs!

Look at his or her work. See if the photographer captured the excitement and emotion of the bridal couple. Also, remember that the wedding album should unfold like a story book of the wedding day.

Consider having a "First Look" session, which is when the bride and groom opt to see each other right before the ceremony. The photographer captures this special, intimate moment, making for beautiful photos. Many couples love First Looks because it puts them at ease before walking down the aisle, as well allows them to skip lengthy portrait sessions between the ceremony and reception. They get to have a private moment together and spend more time with their guests after the ceremony.

When comparing photographer prices, compare the quantity and size of the photographs in your album and the type of album that each photographer will use. Ask how many photos will be taken on average at a wedding of your size. Some photographers do not work with proofs. Rather, they simply supply you with a finished album after the wedding. Doing this may reduce the cost of your album but will also reduce your selection of photographs. Many photographers will put your proofs on a DVD for viewing. This is much less bulky and an easy way to preview all of your wedding photos.

Make sure the photographer you interview is the specific

person who will photograph your wedding. Many companies have more than one photographer. The more professional companies will make sure that you meet with (and view the work of) the photographer who will photograph your wedding. This way you can get an idea of his or her style and personality and begin to establish a rapport with your photographer. Your chosen photographer's name should go on your contract!

Also, some churches do not allow photographs to be shot during the ceremony. Please find out the rules and present them to your photographer so he or she is knowledgeable about your site.

Tips to Save Money: Consider hiring a professional photographer for the formal shots of your ceremony only. You can then ask your guests to take candid shots and create an online photo album where they can post their favorite shots.

Select a photographer who charges a flat fee to shoot the wedding and allows you to purchase the photos on a DVD.

Ask for specials and package deals. Your photographer may be willing to negotiate to get your business, but you won't know if you don't ask.

Price Range: $900 - $9,000

ENGAGEMENT PHOTOS

Many couples are interested in a set of engagement photos to accompany their wedding-day photography. These make a nice keepsake for you, as well as a gift for friends and family. If taken far enough in advance, you can even include these photos in your Save the Date cards.

Options: Most couples prefer to have engagement photos taken outside and not in a studio. Ask your photographer if he or she can scout locations, or you can choose a meaningful spot. Locations like the beach, a favorite outdoor café, your university, a park, a beautiful field, or even your own home make for nice photos. Discuss with your photographer whether you want candid shots or posed portrait shots or a combination of both.

Things to Consider: On the day of the shoot, bring more than one wardrobe change and wear nice shoes, as many shots will be full-body. Engagement shoots usually include affectionate shots such as the couple hugging or even kissing, so talk to your partner about what you're both comfortable with. Finally, ask your photographer to take some classic bridal portraits (shots of just bride).

Modernly, many engagement shoots also include props, such as a picnic blanket, books, balloons, your dog — anything that you can have fun with or that represents you as a couple. Discuss with your bride what you want to incorporate.

Tips to Save Money: Consider hiring the same photographer for engagement photos as for the wedding; many will build the price into the total photography package.

To really cut costs, ask a friend or family member to take photos of you and your fiancée.

Price Range: $75 - $300

NOTES

_____

_____
_____
_____
_____
_____
_____
_____
_____
_____
_____
_____
_____
_____
_____
_____
_____
_____
_____
_____
_____
_____
_____
_____
_____
_____
_____
_____

CEREMONY OFFICIANT

OFFICIANT'S FEE

The officiant's fee is the fee paid to the person who performs your wedding ceremony.

Options: Priest, Clergyman, Minister, Pastor, Chaplain, Rabbi, Judge, Justice of the Peace, or friend or loved one.

Discuss with your officiant the readings you would like incorporated into your ceremony. Some popular readings are:

Beatitudes	Corinthians 13:1-13
Ecclesiastes 3:1-9	Ephesians 3:14-19; 5:1-2
Genesis 1:26-28	Genesis 2:4-9, 15-24
Hosea 2:19-21	Isaiah 61:10I
John 4:7-16	John 15:9-12, 17:22-24
Mark 10:6-9	Proverbs 31:10-31
Romans 12:1-2, 9-18	Ruth 1:16-17
Tobit 8:56-58	

Things to Consider: Some officiants may not accept a fee, depending on your relationship with him or her. If a fee is refused, send a donation to the officiant's church or synagogue.

Tips to Save Money: Have a friend or family member become ordained to perform your ceremony. Simple and inexpensive online programs ($30 and up) are available in every state. Prices and guidelines vary.

Price Range: $100 - $500

OFFICIANT'S GRATUITY

The officiant's gratuity is a discretionary amount of money given to the officiant.

Things to Consider: This amount should depend on your relationship with the officiant and the amount of time he or she spent with you prior to the ceremony.

You should put this fee in a sealed envelope and give it to your best man or wedding consultant, who gives it to the officiant either before or immediately after the ceremony.

Price Range: $50 - $250

UNIQUE CEREMONY IDEAS

IDEAS TO PERSONALIZE YOUR CEREMONY

Regardless of your religious affiliation, there are numerous ways in which you can personalize your wedding ceremony to add a more creative touch. If you're planning a religious ceremony at a church or temple, be sure to discuss all ideas with your officiant.

The following list incorporates some ideas to personalize your wedding ceremony.

- Invite the bride's mother to be part of the processional. Have her walk down the aisle with you and your father. (This is the traditional Jewish processional.)
- Invite your parents to be part of the processional as well.
- Ask friends and family members to perform special readings.
- Incorporate poetry and/or literature into your readings.

- Ask a friend or family member with musical talent to perform at the ceremony.
- Change places with the officiant and face your guests during the ceremony.
- Light a unity candle to symbolize your two lives joining together as one.
- Drink wine from a shared "loving" cup to symbolize bonding with each other.
- Hand a rose to each of your mothers as you pass by them during the recessional.
- Release white doves into the air after being pronounced "husband and wife."
- If the ceremony is held outside on a grassy area, have your guests toss grass or flower seeds over you instead of rice.
- Publicly express gratitude for all that your parents have done for you.
- Use a canopy to designate an altar for a non-church setting. Decorate it in ways that are symbolic or meaningful to you.
- Burn incense to give the ceremony an exotic feeling.

IDEAS TO PERSONALIZE YOUR MARRIAGE VOWS

Regardless of your religious affiliation and whether you're planning a church or outdoor ceremony, there are ways in which you can personalize your marriage vows to make them more meaningful for you. As with all your ceremony plans, be sure to discuss your ideas for marriage vows with your officiant.

The following are some ideas that you might want to consider when planning your marriage vows:

- You and your fiancée could write your own personal marriage vows and keep them secret from one another until the actual ceremony.
- Incorporate your guests and family members into your vows by acknowledging their presence at the ceremony.
- Describe what you cherish most about your partner and what you hope for your future together.
- Describe your commitment to and love for one another.
- Discuss your feelings and beliefs about marriage.
- If either of you has children from a previous marriage, mention these children in your vows and discuss your mutual love for and commitment to them.

NOTES

GIFT REGISTRY

MAIN REGISTRY

Creating the gift registry is something you and your fiancée should work on together. Decide what items you need and what gift items you would like that you might not normally buy for yourselves. You can register for anything from appliances to dishware to gardening supplies to bedding — anything that will help you start your new life together. Register for items in a variety of price ranges, from $20 and up. Guests may want to purchase one big item, combine a few smaller items, or go in on a pricier gift with another wedding guest.

Include gifts from at least two online stores, as well as a retailer that has brick-and-mortar locations, since some guests may want to visit the store and see the items they're purchasing for you in person or avoid paying for shipping and handling.

Your gift registry should never be listed on your wedding

invitations; this is in poor taste. Instead, create a wedding website and list your registry information there, or have the wedding party spread the word to guests.

HONEYMOON REGISTRY

A growing trend in wedding registries is the honeymoon registry. As an alternative to a conventional gift registry, you can create a registry for your honeymoon where guests can help by purchasing a piece of your vacation.

For example, if your honeymoon plane tickets will be $1,000, you might break this into $100 chunks. Or, you might register for things like a $50 bottle of champagne in your hotel room or a $30 snorkeling excursion. A week before your wedding, the registry will close and you will receive a check in the mail for all the items purchased.

A honeymoon registry is great if you don't need a lot of household items; plus, your guests will enjoy contributing to this amazing vacation. Be sure to keep track of who purchased which item and send thank you cards to let guests know how much you enjoyed the activities and amenities they helped purchase.

RECEPTION

The reception is the party where all your guests come together to celebrate your new life as a married couple. It should reflect and complement the formality of your ceremony. The selection of a reception site will depend on its availability, price, proximity to the ceremony site, and the number of people it will accommodate.

As the groom, you may want to coordinate the liquor and/or beverages at the wedding. You will want to consider the kind of bar service you and your fiancée want, the drinks you want to offer, your budget for beverages, and whether you or your caterer will provide alcohol.

Comprehensive information on choosing a reception site, caterer, and food for your reception can be found in the bride's book.

RECEPTION SITE FEE

There are two basic types of reception sites. The first type charges a per person fee that includes the facility, food, tables, silverware, china, and so forth. Examples: hotels, restaurants, and catered yachts. The second type charges a room rental fee and you are responsible for providing the food, beverages, linens, and possibly tables and chairs. Examples: clubs, halls, parks, museums, and private homes.

The advantage of the first type is that almost everything is done for you. The disadvantage, however, is that your choices of food, china, and linen are limited. Usually you are not permitted to bring in an outside caterer and must select from a predetermined menu. Being allowed to bring in your own caterer and alcohol can save a lot of money.

Options: Private homes, gardens, hotels, clubs, restaurants, halls, parks, museums, yachts, and wineries are some of the more popular choices for receptions.

Things to Consider: When comparing the cost of different locations, consider the rental fee, food, beverages, parking, gratuity, setup charges, and the cost of rental equipment needed, such as tables, chairs, canopies, and so forth.

Be sure to get everything included in your price in writing

and ask about extra, hidden fees. If your venue is a hotel ballroom, get the exact room in writing. Some hotels will reserve the right to move your wedding to a smaller room to accommodate another party.

If you are planning an outdoor reception, be sure to rent a tent or have a backup site in case of rain. If the price of a tent is out of your budget, see if there is another couple renting your venue that same weekend who is willing to share the cost with you.

Backyard weddings are very popular for couples with a tight budget because it saves on a rental fee. If a close friend or family member will offer his or her home for your reception, this can be a money-saving option. However, be aware that having a backyard wedding isn't without its costs and caveats. You will need to consider how you will provide or rent tables, chairs, linens, place settings, lighting, a dance floor, parking (if the home doesn't have ample space for parking), restrooms (if the host doesn't want guests inside the home), and space for food prep, cooking and storage. You will also want to be sure the home is covered under the person's homeowner's insurance, in case of an accident. If you do decide to have a backyard wedding however, it can be a memorable and personal reception venue.

Tips to Save Money: Since the cost of the reception is

approximately 35% of the total cost of your wedding, you can save the most money by limiting your guest list. A sit-down dinner can easily cost $100 a head, so cutting just 10 people from your guest list could save $1,000.

Price Range: $300 - $5,000

PARKING FEE/VALET SERVICES

Many reception sites such as hotels, restaurants, etc., charge for parking. It is customary, although not necessary, for the host of the wedding to pay this charge. At a large home reception, you should consider hiring a professional, qualified valet service if parking could be a problem. If so, make sure the valet service is fully insured.

Things to Consider: When comparing the cost of reception sites, don't forget to add the cost of parking to the total price.

Tips to Save Money: To save money, let your guests pay their own parking fees.

Price Range: $3 - $10 per car

LIQUOR/BEVERAGES

Prices for liquor and beverages vary greatly, depending on the amount and brand of alcohol served. Couples may decide to have an alcohol-free wedding or limit the bar to a portion of the event to save money. Traditionally, at least champagne or sparkling cider should be served to toast the couple.

Options: White and red wines, scotch, vodka, gin, rum, and beer are the most popular alcoholic beverages. Soda, lemonade and iced tea are popular nonalcoholic beverages at receptions. And of course, don't forget coffee or tea.

There are a number of options and variations for serving alcoholic beverages: a full open bar where you pay for your guests to drink as much as they wish; an open bar for the first hour, followed by a cash bar where guests pay for their own drinks; cash bar only; beer and wine only; nonalcoholic beverages only; or any combination.

Things to Consider: If you plan to serve alcoholic beverages at a reception site that does not provide liquor, make sure your caterer has a license to serve alcohol and that your reception site allows alcoholic beverages. If you plan to order your own alcohol, do so three or four weeks before the event. If you plan to have a no-host or cash bar, consider notifying your guests so they know to bring cash with them. A simple line that says "No-Host Bar" on the reception card should suffice.

In selecting the type of alcohol to serve, consider the age and preference of your guests, the type of food that will be served, and the time of day your guests will be drinking. Never serve liquor without some type of food.

On average, you should assume one drink per person, per hour at the reception. If you are hosting an open bar at a hotel or restaurant, ask the catering manager how they charge for liquor: by consumption or by number of bottles opened. Get this in writing and ask for a full consumption report after the event.

Lastly, it is not uncommon for the hosts of a party to be held legally responsible for the conduct and safety of their guests. Keep this in mind when planning the quantity and type of beverages to serve. Also, be sure to remind your bartenders not to serve alcohol to minors.

Tips to Save Money: Host alcoholic beverages for the first hour, then go to a cash bar. Or host beer, wine, and soft drinks only and have mixed drinks available on a cash basis. You may also consider having nonalcoholic drinks only, such as a gourmet coffee and tea bar.

Serve one personalized drink instead of a full liquor

selection. Choose something meaningful to you as a couple — the cocktail you drank on your first date, for example. Include a sign at the bar that tells the story of your special drink. You might even include the recipe and a special glass as a favor for guests.

If your caterer allows it, buy liquor from a wholesaler or warehouse store that will let you return unopened bottles.

For the toast, pour champagne only for those guests who ask for it. Many people will make a toast with whatever they are currently drinking.

If some guests won't be drinking alcohol (children, non-drinkers, religious guests), give your caterer or venue a "bar count" instead of a full head count. That way, you won't be charged per guest for alcohol when some won't indulge.

Price Range: $8 - $35 per person

BARTENDING/BAR SETUP FEE

Some reception sites and caterers charge an extra fee for bartending and for setting up the bar.

Tips to Save Money: The bartending fee could be and often is waived if you meet a minimum requirement on beverages consumed. Try to negotiate this with your caterer prior to hiring him or her.

Price Range: $75 - $500

CORKAGE FEE

Many reception sites and caterers make money by marking up the food and alcohol they sell. You may wish to provide your own alcohol for several reasons. First, it is more cost effective. Second, you may want to serve an exotic wine or champagne that the reception site or caterer does not offer. In either case, be prepared to pay a corkage fee. This is the fee for each bottle brought into the reception site and opened by a member of their staff.

Things to Consider: You need to consider whether the expenses saved after paying the corkage fee justify the hassle and liability of bringing in your own alcohol.

Price Range: $5 - $20 per bottle

FEE TO POUR COFFEE

In addition to corkage and cake-cutting fees, some facilities also charge extra to pour coffee with the wedding cake.

Things to Consider: Again, when comparing the cost of various reception sites, don't forget to add up all the extra miscellaneous costs, such as the fee for pouring coffee.

Price Range: $0.25 - $1 per person

GRATUITY

It is customary to pay a gratuity fee to your caterer. The average gratuity is 20 percent of your food and beverage bill.

Tips to Save Money: Ask about these costs up front and select your caterer or reception site accordingly.

Price Range: 15 - 20% of total food and beverage bill

NOTES

_____

_____

_____

_____

_____

_____

_____

_____

_____

_____

_____

_____

_____

_____

_____

_____

_____

_____

_____

_____

_____

_____

_____

_____

_____

_____

_____

_____

RECEPTION MUSIC

You will need to hire musicians, a band or a DJ to play music at your reception and keep guests dancing and having a good time. When you select music for your reception, keep in mind the age and musical preference of your guests, your budget, and any restrictions that the reception site may have. Bands and musicians are typically more expensive than DJs.

Options: You need to find a reliable DJ, band, or combination of instruments and vocalists who will play the type of music you want and keep guests feeling upbeat all night. They should have experience performing at wedding receptions so they understand the flow of the event and can hopefully act as your master of ceremonies.

Things to Consider: If you want your musician to be your MC, make sure he or she has a complete timeline for your reception in order to announce the various events, such as the toasts, first dance, and cutting of the cake.

If you need a large variety of music to satisfy all your guests, consider hiring a DJ. Sit down with your fiancée and decide on a list of the songs you want played at your reception and the sequence in which you want them played. You may also want to provide a "Do Not Play" list of songs you don't want the DJ to play, even if they are requested.

If you choose a live band, consider watching your musicians perform at another event before booking their services. You should provide them with a few modern songs you would like at your reception and see if they are able to play them. You should also find out if you need to provide prerecorded music to play while the musicians take a break during the reception.

You should consider whether you want to hire a regular DJ or an entertainer — a DJ who can also provide things like disco dance lessons for the crowd or a light show. Some DJs interact with the crowd much more than others. Decide which type of DJ you want.

Be sure to check with your reception venue about any music restrictions. Some venues located in residential areas, for instance, may have a rule that music has to be off by 10 p.m. Consider this when you choosing a venue, as well.

Tips to Save Money: A DJ is typically less expensive than a "live" musician. Some facilities have contracts with certain DJs, and you may be able to save money by hiring one of them.

When you hold your wedding can also help you save money on your reception music. DJs and bands may charge 10 to 20 percent more for a Saturday night wedding. Additionally, booking a DJ near the holidays or on New Year's Eve can nearly double the price!

Check the music department of local colleges and universities for names of student musicians and DJs. You may be able to hire a student for a fraction of the price of a professional musician or DJ.

Price Range: $500 - $5,000

NOTES

BAKERY

WEDDING CAKE

Options: When ordering your cake, you will have to decide not only on a flavor, but also on a size, shape, and color. The most common flavors are chocolate, carrot, lemon, and vanilla cake. Add a filling to your cake, such as mousse, custard, ganache or a fruit filling.

You and your fiancée should meet with bakers who offer free cake tastings so you can choose the flavors, icings and fillings you like best. If you can't agree on one flavor, have tiers of different flavors.

Things to Consider: Icing types and toppings vary the price and look of the cake. Fondant provides a smooth, satiny look and doesn't need refrigeration, making it very popular, although it is one of the most expensive icings and the taste is not always great. Marzipan is a paste made from ground almonds and sugar, which is a better-tasting alternative to fondant. It can also be molded into flowers and other decorations. Ganache and buttercream are also popular icings that are lighter and taste great, although they melt easily and may not be the best choice for outdoor weddings. Sugar gum paste is another type of icing that your baker can use to create figurines, flowers, shapes, and more.

Price Range: **$2 - $12 per piece**

GROOM'S CAKE

The groom's cake is traditionally a chocolate cake decorated with fruit, but modernly, this small cake reflects the groom's interests, such as a favorite hobby or sports team.

In this old Southern tradition, the groom's cake is cut up and distributed to guests in little boxes marked with the bride and groom's names. Today, the groom's cake, if offered, is cut and served along with the wedding cake.

Tips to Save Money: Because of its cost and the labor involved in cutting and distributing the cake, many couples skip this custom.

Price Range: **$1 - $2 per piece**

FLOWERS

GROOM'S BOUTONNIERE

The groom wears his boutonniere on the left lapel, nearest to his heart.

Options: Boutonnieres for men in the wedding party are generally a single blossom, such as a rosebud, calla lily, freesia, or a miniature carnation. If a single bud is used for the wedding party, the groom can wear two buds, or add a sprig of greenery, to differentiate himself from the groomsmen.

Things to Consider: Be careful when using alstroemeria as a boutonniere, as its sap can be harmful if it enters the bloodstream.

Tips to Save Money: Ask your florist which flowers will be cost-effective for boutonnieres, such as mini carnations instead of roses.

Or, make your own boutonnieres out of non-floral materials, such as feathers, shells, felt, buttons and more. Work with a theme, such as fishing, golf, etc.

Price Range: $4 - $25

USHERS/FAMILY MEMBERS' BOUTONNIERES

Each man in the wedding party should have a boutonniere to wear on his left lapel. The officiant, if male, may also be given a boutonniere to reflect his important role in the ceremony. The ring bearer may or may not wear a boutonniere.

Options: Boutonnieres are generally a single blossom, such as a rosebud, calla lily, freesia, or a miniature carnation.

Things to Consider: The groom should also consider ordering boutonnieres for other close family members such as fathers, grandfathers, and brothers. Your male family members will feel more included in your wedding and it will let guests know that they are family.

Tips to Save Money: Ask your florist which flowers will be cost-effective, or make your own boutonnieres out of non-floral materials, such as feathers, shells, felt, buttons, golf tees, and more.

Price Range: $3 - $15

FEMALE FAMILY MEMBERS' CORSAGES

The groom is responsible for providing flowers for his mother, the bride's mother, and the grandmothers. The officiant, if female, may also be given a corsage to reflect her important role in the ceremony. The corsages don't have to be identical, but they should be coordinated with the color of their dresses.

Options: You may order flowers that can be pinned to a lapel or worn around a wrist. You should ask which style the women prefer, and if a particular color is needed to coordinate with their dresses. Gardenias, camellias, white orchids, or cymbidium orchids are excellent choices for corsages, as they go well with any outfit.

Things to Consider: You may also want to consider ordering corsages for other close family members, such as sisters and aunts. This will add a little to your floral expenses but will make these female family members feel more included in your wedding and will let guests know that they are related to you and the bride. Many women do not like to wear corsages, so check with the people involved before ordering the flowers.

Tips to Save Money: Ask your florist to recommend reasonable flowers for corsages that coordinate with the bride's bouquet. Dendrobium orchids are well-priced and make lovely corsages.

Using silk flowers and non-floral objects can also be a way to save money. Talk to your fiancée about any DIY projects you both wish to take on.

Price Range: $10 - $35

TRANSPORTATION

Transportation to and from the ceremony and reception is another aspect of the wedding the groom can handle. It is customary for the bride and her father to ride to the ceremony site together on the wedding day. You may also include some or all members of her wedding party. If desired, you can provide a second vehicle for the rest of the attendants. The bride and her father will go in the last vehicle. This vehicle will also be used to transport the bride and groom to the reception site after the ceremony.

Options: There are various options for transportation. The most popular choice is a limousine, since it is large and open and can accommodate many people, as well as your bridal gown. If you would like to ride with your entire wedding party, consider riding in style in a trendy stretch-Hummer limo.

You can also choose to rent a car that symbolizes your personality as a couple. You might rent a luxury car, such as a Mercedes or Ferrari, or a vintage vehicle, such as a 1950s Thunderbird or 1930s Cadillac. You can rent a luxury or antique car for about $125 a day, and ask a friend or family member to act as the driver.

If your ceremony and reception sites are fairly close together, and if weather permits, you might want to consider a horse-drawn carriage. This is a very elegant and special way to arrive in style; however, you should check with the venue to make sure their location can accommodate the carriage. For instance, if you are getting married in a big city, it may be a traffic obstruction to have a carriage.

Things to Consider: Consider hiring only one large limousine. This limousine can transport you, your parents, and your attendants to the ceremony, and then you and the bride from the ceremony to the reception.

Always make sure the transportation company you choose is fully licensed and has liability insurance.

Get everything in writing before your wedding, including exact pickup times, requests for items like champagne glasses and ice, and the license plate number of the exact vehicle you want for your wedding day. Some companies will sell you with one vehicle and attempt to substitute a different vehicle on the actual day.

Don't forget to factor in the driver's gratuity when you

price out transportation options. Drivers typically get a 15 to 20 percent tip, in addition to the hourly rental rate.

Tips to Save Money: If you're not traveling far to the ceremony and reception venues, it may not make sense to pay for transportation, especially since limousines are typically booked on a three-hour-minimum basis.

Lastly, see if you have a family member or friend with an interesting car who wouldn't mind lending it to you for the wedding day.

Price Range: $35 - $200 per hour

NOTES

GIFTS

Gifts are a wonderful way to show appreciation to family, friends, members of your wedding party, and to all those who have assisted you in your wedding planning process. Brides and grooms usually like to exchange something small yet meaningful. Keepsake items make wonderful gifts for members of the wedding party.

BRIDE'S GIFT

The bride's gift is traditionally given by the groom to the bride. It is typically a personal gift, such as a piece of jewelry.

Options: A string of pearls, a watch, pearl earrings, jewelry box, perfume, or beautiful lingerie are nice gifts for the bride from her groom.

Things to Consider: This gift is not necessary and should be given only if your budget allows.

Tips to Save Money: Consider omitting this gift. A handwritten letter is a very special, yet inexpensive gift.

Price Range: $50 - $500

USHERS' GIFTS

Ushers' gifts are given by the groom to his ushers as a permanent keepsake of the wedding.

Options: For ushers' gifts, consider something they can wear during and after the wedding, such as a watch or cufflinks.

Other great gifts include a leather wallet, money clip, cigars, a personalized flask, luxury shaving kit, or a bottle of fine wine.

Things to Consider: The groom should deliver his gifts to the ushers at the bachelor party or at the rehearsal dinner. The gift to the best man may be similar to the ushers' gifts, but should be a bit more expensive.

Tips to Save Money: Buy your ushers ties for the wedding. Nice ties can be inexpensive at stores like Marshall's and Nordstrom Rack, and ushers will wear them again.

Price Range: $20 - $200 per gift

PARTIES

Weddings are often much more than a day-long celebration. Some traditional events include the engagement party, bridal shower, bachelor and bachelorette parties, bridesmaids' luncheon, and rehearsal dinner. Some couples also like to have a brunch the day after the wedding to relax and relive the previous evening's celebration. You should include whatever celebrations fall within your budget.

ENGAGEMENT PARTY

The engagement party is generally thrown a few months after the announcement of the engagement and is hosted by either the bride's or groom's family to celebrate and allow the families the get acquainted.

The guest list for the engagement party should be limited to friends and family who will be invited to the wedding. Do not invite anyone who won't receive a wedding invitation. However, that doesn't mean that everyone you plan to have on your wedding day guest list should be invited. An engagement party is a smaller, more intimate affair for your families and closest friends.

Gifts are not required at this party, although some guests may bring them anyhow.

Options: An engagement party is typically held in your parents' home; however, renting a space or having dinner in a nice restaurant are also acceptable.

Consider anything from a 5-course meal to a backyard barbecue to hors d'oeuvres and cocktails to a buffet-style meal at a restaurant. You may want to reflect the formality of your wedding in the engagement party, or you may want it to be very casual.

Things to Consider: If your families have never met, you will want to plan some ice breakers and be sure that the type of party you choose allows for lots of conversation. For example, a formal sit-down dinner may not be the most comfortable atmosphere for people getting to know each other.

Tips to Save Money: If your schedule or budget won't allow for it, an engagement party is by no means a requirement.

BACHELOR PARTY

The bachelor party is a men-only affair typically organized by your best man. He is responsible for selecting the date and reserving the place and entertainment, as well as inviting your male friends and family. Your best man should also assign responsibilities to your ushers as they should help with the organization of the bachelor party.

Options: A bachelor party can be as simple as a group of guys getting together for dinner and drinks, a day of golfing, a casino day trip, or a cruise. You might also attend a sporting event, brewery tour or tasting, or be adventurous and go skydiving or camping.

Be sure to tell your best man the type of party you want — mild or wild. Whatever you plan, be respectful of your bride when you're celebrating at your bachelor party!

Things to Consider: You often hear wild stories about bachelor parties being nights full of women and alcohol, however, these types of events are actually quite rare. The bachelor party is simply a night for great friends and family to celebrate together.

Your best man should not plan your bachelor party for the night before the wedding, since you may consume a fair amount of alcohol and stay up late. You don't want to have a hangover or be exhausted during your wedding. Have the bachelor party two or three nights or even several months before the wedding.

Your best man should designate a driver for you and for those who will be drinking. Remember, you and your best man are responsible for the well-being of everybody invited to the party.

Whatever you do, make this party a memorable one! Do something different and spend quality time with your friends and family members.

Tips to Save Money: Instead of spending a lot of money to fly and stay in another city, have the bachelor party in the same city as the wedding, in the days leading up to the event.

REHEARSAL DINNER

The groom's parents customarily host a dinner party following the rehearsal, the evening before the wedding. The dinner usually includes the bridal party, their spouses or guests, both sets of parents, close family members, the officiant, and the wedding consultant and/or coordinator. You may also invite out-of-town guests who have traveled a long way to the wedding, if budget permits.

Instead of an intimate sit-down dinner, you may consider having a welcome night for all your guests with cocktails and hors d'oeurves.

Options: The rehearsal dinner can be held just about anywhere, from a restaurant, hotel, or private hall to the groom's parents' home.

Things to Consider: The evening will be about dinner, chatting with friends and family, getting to know the other side of the family better, and thanking all the important people who have contributed to your wedding.

Toasts are traditionally given by the groom's father and the bride and groom. The groom's father will toast his new daughter and her family, and the couple should thank their guests for coming and their families for their help.

The rehearsal dinner is also the time to give the wedding party their gifts and to thank them, as well.

Tips to Save Money: Try going to a restaurant that specializes in Mexican food, Chinese or gourmet pizza for a fun and inexpensive option for a casual rehearsal dinner.

NOTES

LEGAL MATTERS

MARRIAGE LICENSE

Marriage license requirements are state-regulated and may be obtained from the County Clerk in most county courthouses or online at www.usmarriagelaws.com.

Some states (California and Nevada, for example) offer two types of marriage licenses: a public license and a confidential one. The public license is the most common one and requires a health certificate. This license can only be obtained at the County Clerk's office.

The confidential license is usually less expensive and does not require a health certificate. If offered, it can usually be obtained from most Justices of the Peace. An oath must be taken in order to receive either license.

Requirements vary from state to state but generally include the following points:

1. Applying for and paying the fee for the marriage license. There is usually a waiting period before the license is valid and a limited time before it expires.

2. Meeting residency requirements of the state and/or county where the ceremony will take place.

3. Meeting the legal age requirements for both bride and groom or having parental consent.

4. Presenting any required identification, birth or baptismal certificates, marriage eligibility or other documents.

5. Obtaining a medical examination and/or blood test for both the bride and groom to detect communicable diseases.

NAME & ADDRESS CHANGE

Don't forget that if you are moving into a new home after the wedding, you will need to submit your address change to your credit card companies, insurance providers, billing companies and more. In addition, you and your fiancée may want to talk about opening a joint checking account, adding her name to checks and billing statements, and more.

TOASTS

It is customary for your best man to offer a toast at the reception to introduce himself, the wedding party, and the newly married couple. This is followed by the groom thanking his best man and then toasting his bride and both sets of parents.

After the groom's toast, anybody else can offer a toast. Typically, the father of the bride and the maid of honor offer a toast.

The toast begins after the receiving line breaks up at a cocktail reception or before dinner during a dinner reception. Toasts can also be offered after the main course or after the cake is served.

Your toast could be to express thanks to everybody involved in planning the wedding or to give thanks to those who traveled long distances to come to your wedding. It can be serious, such as expressing how much you love your new wife; or it can be funny, such as describing how your fiancée played "hard to get" when you two first met.

Your toast should not be so short that it sounds rude, or so long that your guests get bored. During the toast, everyone rises except those who are being toasted. And no one should drink from their cup until after the toast. After you finish your toast, raise your glass toward the person or persons being toasted.

Your toast should sound sincere and not overly rehearsed. However, it is a good idea to practice it beforehand. If you are anxious about speaking in public, you may want to write yourself a few notes on an index card or practice your speech for your best man. If you are still very nervous, keep your speech short and to the point.

DO'S & DON'TS

Your wedding will last only a few hours but will likely take several months to plan. That is why it is so important to enjoy the complete wedding planning process. This is a time to get excited, fall even more deeply in love with each other, learn more about each other, and learn how to give and take. If you can handle your wedding planning with your fiancée and parents, you can handle anything! Here is a list of do's and don'ts when planning your special day. If you follow these suggestions, your wedding planning will be more enjoyable and the wedding itself will be much more smooth and beautiful.

DO'S

- Help your bride make decisions and talk to vendors as often as you can.

- Consult a professional wedding planner.

DO'S & DON'TS

- Maintain a sense of humor.

- Maintain open communication with your fiancée and both sets of parents, especially if they are financing all or part of the wedding.

- Be receptive to your parents' ideas, especially if they are financing all or part of the wedding.

- Give your bride plenty of feedback, when asked. Never say, "I don't care"!

- Keep your overall budget in mind.

- Buy *Wedding Party Responsibility Cards*, published by Wedding Solutions Publishing, and give one to each member of your wedding party.

- Purchase a complete wedding planner to keep track of vendors, appointments and more. Consider *Easy Wedding Planning Plus* or any other of the 16 best-selling wedding planning books published by Wedding Solutions.

- Register for gifts; consider a price range that your guests can afford.

- Do something to let your family members stand out

at the wedding, such as giving a rose to each of your mothers as you walk down the aisle.

- Break in your shoes well before your wedding day.

- Check recent references for all of your service providers.

- Get everything in writing with your service providers.

- Assign your guests to tables and group them together by age, interest, acquaintances, etc.

- Don't be late! You don't want to keep guests waiting!

- Try to spend some time with each of your guests and personally thank them for coming to your wedding.

- Encourage the bride's parents to introduce their family and friends to the family and friends of the groom's family, and vice-versa.

- Toast both sets of parents at the rehearsal dinner and/ or at the reception. Thank them for everything they have done to help give you a beautiful wedding.

- Keep a smile on your face; there will be many photographs taken of you.

- Eat at the reception, especially if you will be drinking alcohol. If you don't have much time, ask your caterer to set aside a plate for you and your fiancée.

- Preserve the top tier of your wedding cake for your first year anniversary.

- Expect something to go wrong on your wedding day. Relax and don't let it bother you! Help your bride keep things in perspective.

- Assign someone to collect things like your guest book, toasting glasses and anything you want to save.

- Send a special gift to both sets of parents after the wedding, such as a small album. Personalize this gift by having it engraved.

DON'TS

- Don't be controlling. Be open to other people's ideas.

- Don't get involved in other activities; you will be very busy planning your wedding.

- Don't make any major decisions without discussing them openly with your fiancée.

- Don't overspend your budget!

- Don't wait until the last minute to hire your service providers. The good ones get booked months in advance.

- Don't try to make everybody happy. Decide what aspects of the wedding are most important to you both.

- Don't try to impress your friends.

- Don't invite old girlfriends to your wedding; you don't want to make your bride feel uncomfortable.

- Don't take on too much. Delegate responsibilities to your fiancée, your parents, and to members of your wedding party.

- Don't rely on friends or family to take your wedding photographs. Hire a professional.

- Don't keep guests waiting too long between the ceremony and reception. Consider taking photos before the ceremony or limiting photos to 30 minutes.

- Don't assume that members of your wedding party know what to do. Give each of them a copy of the *Wedding Party Responsibility Cards*.

- Don't assume that your service providers know what to do. Give them a timeline or schedule of your event.

- Don't schedule your bachelor party the night before the wedding. You don't want to have a hangover on your special day.

- Don't get drunk at your reception. And don't drive if you have had too much to drink.

- Don't rub cake in your bride's face during the cake-cutting ceremony; she may not appreciate it!

- Don't give your groomsmen the keys to your bridal suite or they may play a prank on you. Give a key to the maid of honor so she can decorate the room with champagne and flowers.

- Don't forget to get or renew your passports several months before an international honeymoon.

- Don't leave your reception without saying goodbye to family and friends.

WEDDING PARTY RESPONSIBILITIES

Each member of your wedding party has his own individual duties and responsibilities, as this chapter explains.

The most convenient method for conveying this information to members of your wedding party is by purchasing a set of *Wedding Party Responsibility Cards*, published by WS Publishing Group.

These cards are attractive and contain all the information your wedding party needs to know to assure a smooth wedding: what to do, how to do it, when to do it, when to arrive, and much more. They also include financial responsibilities as well as the processional, recessional, and altar lineup. This book is available at most major bookstores.

BEST MAN

- Responsible for organizing ushers' activities.
- Organize bachelor party for groom.
- Drive groom to ceremony site and see that he is properly dressed before the wedding.
- Arrive dressed at ceremony site one hour before the wedding for photographs.
- Bring marriage license to wedding.
- Pay the clergyman, musicians, photographer, and any other service providers the day of the wedding.
- Witness the signing of the marriage license.
- Drive newlyweds to reception, if no hired driver.
- Offer first toast at reception, usually before dinner.
- Keep groom on schedule.
- Dance with maid of honor during the bridal party dance.
- May drive couple to airport or honeymoon suite.
- Oversee return of tuxedo rentals for groom and ushers, on time and in good condition.

USHERS

- Help best man with bachelor party.
- Arrive dressed at ceremony site one hour before the wedding for photographs.

- Distribute wedding programs and maps to the reception as guests arrive.
- Two ushers may roll carpet down the aisle after both mothers are seated.
- Seat guests at the ceremony as follows:
  - If female, offer the right arm.
  - If male, walk along his left side.
  - If couple, offer right arm to female; male follows a step or two behind.
  - Seat bride's guests in left pews.
  - Seat groom's guests in right pews.
  - Maintain equal number of guests in left and right pews, if possible.
  - If a group of guests arrive at the same time, seat the eldest woman first.
  - Just prior to the processional, escort groom's mother to her seat; then escort bride's mother to her seat.
- If pew ribbons are used, two ushers may loosen them one row at a time after the ceremony.
- Direct guests to the reception site.
- Dance with bridesmaids and other important guests.

GROOM'S MOTHER

- Help prepare guest list for groom and his family.
- Select attire that complements mother of the bride's attire.

- Make accommodations for groom's out-of-town guests.
- With groom's father, plan rehearsal dinner.
- Arrive dressed at ceremony site one hour before the wedding for photographs.
- May stand up to signal the start of the processional.
- Can witness the signing of the marriage license.

GROOM'S FATHER

- Help prepare guest list for groom and family.
- Select attire that complements groom's attire.
- With groom's mother, plan rehearsal dinner.
- Offer toast to bride at rehearsal dinner.
- Arrive dressed at ceremony site one hour before the wedding for photographs.
- Can witness the signing of the marriage license.

TIMELINES

The following section includes two different timelines or schedule of events for your wedding day: one for members of your wedding party and one for the various service providers you have hired. Use these timelines to help your wedding party and service providers understand their roles and where they need to be throughout your wedding day. This will also give you a much better idea of how your special day will unfold.

When preparing your timeline, first list the time that your wedding ceremony will begin. Then work forward or backwards, using the sample as your guide. The samples included give you an idea of how much time each event typically takes. But feel free to change the amount of time allotted for any event when customizing your own.

SAMPLE WEDDING PARTY TIMELINE

This is a sample wedding party timeline. To develop your own, use the blank form in this chapter, then make copies and give one to each member of your wedding party.

TIME	DESCRIPTION	BRIDE	BRIDE'S MOTHER	BRIDE'S FATHER	MAID OF HONOR	BRIDESMAIDS	BRIDE'S FAMILY	GROOM	GROOM'S MOTHER	GROOM'S FATHER	BEST MAN	USHERS	GROOM'S FAMILY	FLOWER GIRL	RING BEARER
2:30 PM	Hair/makeup appointment	✓	✓		✓	✓									
4:30 PM	Arrive at dressing site							✓			✓	✓			
5:15 PM	Arrive at ceremony site							✓	✓	✓	✓	✓	✓		
5:15 PM	Pre-ceremony photos	✓	✓	✓	✓	✓	✓								
5:30 PM	Ushers distribute wedding programs											✓			
5:30 PM	Prelude music begins														
5:45 PM	Ushers seat honored guests											✓			
5:50 PM	Ushers seat groom's parents								✓	✓		✓			
5:55 PM	Ushers seat bride's mother		✓									✓			
5:55 PM	Attendants line up for procession			✓	✓							✓		✓	✓
5:56 PM	Bride's father takes his place next to bride	✓		✓											
5:58 PM	Groom's party enters							✓			✓				
6:00 PM	Processional music begins														

TIME	DESCRIPTION	BRIDE	BRIDE'S MOTHER	BRIDE'S FATHER	MAID OF HONOR	BRIDESMAIDS	BRIDE'S FAMILY	GROOM	GROOM'S MOTHER	GROOM'S FATHER	BEST MAN	USHERS	GROOM'S FAMILY	FLOWER GIRL	RING BEARER
6:20 PM	Wedding party marches down aisle	✓			✓			✓			✓			✓	✓
6:25 PM	Sign marriage certificate	✓			✓			✓			✓				
6:30 PM	Post-ceremony photos taken	✓	✓	✓	✓	✓	✓	✓	✓	✓	✓	✓	✓	✓	✓
6:30 PM	Cocktails and hors d'oeuvres served														
7:45 PM	Guests are seated and dinner is served														
8:30 PM	Toasts are given										✓				
8:40 PM	First dance	✓						✓							
9:40 PM	Cake-cutting ceremony	✓						✓							
10:00 PM	Bride tosses bouquet to single women	✓			✓	✓								✓	
10:10 PM	Groom removes garter from bride's leg	✓						✓							
10:15 PM	Groom tosses garter to single men							✓			✓	✓			✓
10:45 PM	Bride and groom make grand exit	✓						✓							

WEDDING PARTY TIMELINE

Create your own timeline using this form. Make copies and give one to each member of your wedding party.

TIME	DESCRIPTION	BRIDE	BRIDE'S MOTHER	BRIDE'S FATHER	MAID OF HONOR	BRIDESMAIDS	BRIDE'S FAMILY	GROOM	GROOM'S MOTHER	GROOM'S FATHER	BEST MAN	USHERS	GROOM'S FAMILY	FLOWER GIRL	RING BEARER

TIME	DESCRIPTION	BRIDE	BRIDE'S MOTHER	BRIDE'S FATHER	MAID OF HONOR	BRIDESMAIDS	BRIDE'S FAMILY	GROOM	GROOM'S MOTHER	GROOM'S FATHER	BEST MAN	USHERS	GROOM'S FAMILY	FLOWER GIRL	RING BEARER

SAMPLE SERVICE PROVIDER TIMELINE

This is a sample of a service provider timeline. To develop your own, use the blank form in this chapter, then make copies and give one to each one of your service providers.

TIME	DESCRIPTION	BAKER	CATERER	CEREMONY MUSICIANS	OTHER	FLORIST	HAIRSTYLIST	MAKEUP ARTIST	PARTY RENTALS	PHOTOGRAPHER	RECEPTION MUSICIANS	VIDEOGRAPHER
1:00 PM	Supplies delivered to ceremony site								✓			
1:30 PM	Supplies delivered to reception site								✓			
2:30 PM	Makeup artist meets bride at:							✓				
3:00 PM	Hairstylist meets bride at:						✓					
4:15 PM	Caterer begins setting up		✓									
4:40 PM	Baker delivers cake to reception site	✓										
4:45 PM	Pre-ceremony photos of groom's family at:									✓		
5:00 PM	Videographer arrives at ceremony site											✓
5:15 PM	Pre-ceremony photos of bride's family at:									✓		
5:20 PM	Ceremony site decorations finalized				✓	✓						
5:30 PM	Prelude music begins			✓								
5:45 PM	Reception site decorations finalized		✓		✓	✓						
6:30 PM	Post-ceremony photos at:									✓		
6:30 PM	Band or DJ begins playing										✓	

SAMPLE SERVICE PROVIDER TIMELINE

TIME	DESCRIPTION	BAKER	CATERER	CEREMONY MUSICIANS	OTHER	FLORIST	HAIRSTYLIST	LIMOUSINE	PARTY RENTALS	PHOTOGRAPHER	RECEPTION MUSICIANS	VIDEOGRAPHER
6:30 PM	Transport guest book/gifts to reception site				✓							
6:45 PM	Move arch/urns/flowers to reception site				✓							
7:00 PM	Limo picks up bride/groom at ceremony site							✓				
7:15 PM	DJ announces entrance of bride and groom										✓	
7:45 PM	Dinner is served		✓									
8:15 PM	Champagne served for toasts		✓									
8:30 PM	Band/DJ announces toast by best man										✓	
8:40 PM	Band/DJ announces first dance										✓	
9:00 PM	Transport gifts to:				✓							
9:30 PM	Band/DJ announces cake-cutting ceremony										✓	
10:30 PM	Transport top tier of cake, cake-top, etc. to:				✓							
10:40 PM	Transport rental items to:				✓							
10:45 PM	Limo picks up bride/groom at reception site							✓				
11:45 PM	Picks up supplies at ceremony/reception sites								✓			

SAMPLE SERVICE PROVIDER TIMELINE

This is a sample of a service provider timeline. To develop your own, use the blank form in this chapter, then make copies and give one to each one of your service providers.

TIME	DESCRIPTION	BAKER	CATERER	CEREMONY MUSICIANS	OTHER	FLORIST	HAIRSTYLIST	MAKEUP ARTIST	PARTY RENTALS	PHOTOGRAPHER	RECEPTION MUSICIANS	VIDEOGRAPHER
1:00 PM	Supplies delivered to ceremony site								✓			
1:30 PM	Supplies delivered to reception site								✓			
2:30 PM	Makeup artist meets bride at:							✓				
3:00 PM	Hairstylist meets bride at:						✓					
4:15 PM	Caterer begins setting up		✓									
4:40 PM	Baker delivers cake to reception site	✓										
4:45 PM	Pre-ceremony photos of groom's family at:									✓		
5:00 PM	Videographer arrives at ceremony site											✓
5:15 PM	Pre-ceremony photos of bride's family at:									✓		
5:20 PM	Ceremony site decorations finalized				✓	✓						
5:30 PM	Prelude music begins			✓								
5:45 PM	Reception site decorations finalized		✓		✓	✓						
6:30 PM	Post-ceremony photos at:									✓		
6:30 PM	Band or DJ begins playing										✓	

TIME	DESCRIPTION	BAKER	CATERER	CEREMONY MUSICIANS	OTHER	FLORIST	HAIRSTYLIST	LIMOUSINE	PARTY RENTALS	PHOTOGRAPHER	RECEPTION MUSICIANS	VIDEOGRAPHER
6:30 PM	Transport guest book/gifts to reception site				✓							
6:45 PM	Move arch/urns/flowers to reception site				✓							
7:00 PM	Limo picks up bride/groom at ceremony site							✓				
7:15 PM	DJ announces entrance of bride and groom										✓	
7:45 PM	Dinner is served		✓									
8:15 PM	Champagne served for toasts		✓									
8:30 PM	Band/DJ announces toast by best man										✓	
8:40 PM	Band/DJ announces first dance										✓	
9:00 PM	Transport gifts to:				✓							
9:30 PM	Band/DJ announces cake-cutting ceremony										✓	
10:30 PM	Transport top tier of cake, cake-top, etc. to:				✓							
10:40 PM	Transport rental items to:				✓							
10:45 PM	Limo picks up bride/groom at reception site							✓				
11:45 PM	Picks up supplies at ceremony/reception sites								✓			

SERVICE PROVIDER TIMELINE

Create your own timeline using this form. Make copies and give one to each of your service providers.

TIME	DESCRIPTION	BAKER	CATERER	CEREMONY MUSICIANS	OFFICIANT	OTHER	FLORIST	HAIRSTYLIST	LIMOUSINE	MAKEUP ARTIST	MANICURIST	PARTY RENTALS	PHOTOGRAPHER	RECEPTION MUSICIANS	VIDEOGRAPHER

TIME	DESCRIPTION	BAKER	CATERER	CEREMONY MUSICIANS	OFFICIANT	OTHER	FLORIST	HAIRSTYLIST	LIMOUSINE	MAKEUP ARTIST	MANICURIST	PARTY RENTALS	PHOTOGRAPHER	RECEPTION MUSICIANS	VIDEOGRAPHER

NOTES

WHO PAYS FOR WHAT

GROOM AND/OR GROOM'S FAMILY

- Own travel expenses and attire
- Rehearsal dinner
- Wedding gift for bridal couple
- Bride's wedding ring
- Gifts for groom's attendants
- Medical exam for groom including blood test
- Bride's bouquet and going away corsage
- Mothers' and grandmothers' corsages
- All boutonnieres
- Officiant's fee
- Marriage license
- Honeymoon expenses (traditionally)

ATTENDANTS

- Own attire except boutonnieres
- Travel expenses
- Bachelor party paid for by best man and ushers
- Wedding gift for bridal couple

NOTES

WEDDING FORMATIONS

The following section illustrates the typical ceremony formations (Processional, Recessional and Altar Line Up) for both Christian and Jewish weddings, as well as the typical formations for the Receiving Line, Head Table and Parents' Tables at the reception.

*A*LTAR *L*INE *U*P

ABBREVIATIONS

B=Bride GF=Groom's Father G=Groom
BM=Best Man BMa=Bridesmaids MH=Maid of Honor
BF=Bride's Father OR=Other Relatives BMo=Bride's Mother
O=Officiant U=Ushers GM=Groom's Mother

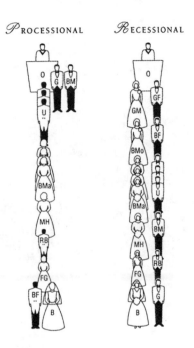

𝒫ROCESSIONAL   ℛECESSIONAL

ABBREVIATIONS

B=Bride	GF=Groom's Father	G=Groom
BM=Best Man	BMa=Bridesmaids	MH=Maid of Honor
BF=Bride's Father	OR=Other Relatives	BMo=Bride's Mother
O=Officiant	U=Ushers	GM=Groom's Mother

$\mathscr{A}$LTAR $\mathscr{L}$INE $\mathscr{U}$P

ABBREVIATIONS

B=Bride   GF=Groom's Father   G=Groom
BM=Best Man   BMa=Bridesmaids   MH=Maid of Honor
BF=Bride's Father   OR=Other Relatives   BMo=Bride's Mother
O=Officiant   U=Ushers   GM=Groom's Mother

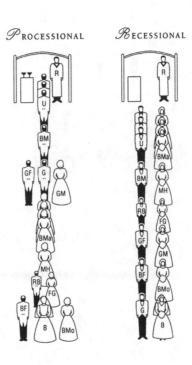

*P*ROCESSIONAL   *R*ECESSIONAL

ABBREVIATIONS

B=Bride	GF=Groom's Father	G=Groom
BM=Best Man	BMa=Bridesmaids	MH=Maid of Honor
BF=Bride's Father	OR=Other Relatives	BMo=Bride's Mother
O=Officiant	U=Ushers	GM=Groom's Mother

ℛECEIVING ℒINE

ℋEAD 𝒯ABLE

𝒫ARENTS' 𝒯ABLE

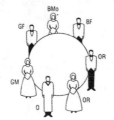

ABBREVIATIONS

B=Bride	GF=Groom's Father	G=Groom
BM=Best Man	BMa=Bridesmaids	MH=Maid of Honor
BF=Bride's Father	OR=Other Relatives	BMo=Bride's Mother
O=Officiant	U=Ushers	GM=Groom's Mother

HONEYMOON

Your honeymoon is the time to celebrate your new life together as a married couple and fall even more in love. It will be the vacation of a lifetime. The honeymoon was traditionally paid for by the groom, but with modern honeymoons costing an average of $4,000, it is more common for both the bride and groom to contribute.

Don't wait to start planning your honeymoon! Deciding where to go and what to do is a process that can take several weeks or months.

Maybe your idea of a perfect honeymoon is ten days of adventure, sightseeing and discovery, but for your fiancée, it may be ten days of resting in a beach chair and romantic strolls in the evening. You should work together to decide on the activities and setting you want, as well as to create a honeymoon budget.

There are many types of traditional and nontraditional honeymoons to consider. Laid-back tropical-island honeymoons to the Caribbean and Hawaii are extremely popular, as are winter honeymoons in places like Canada and Alaska. Many couples also choose a honeymoon of dancing, gambling and golf in Las Vegas.

Cruises are a very popular choice. You get to visit a wide variety of places in a short amount of time and prices generally include almost every amenity, other than items like alcoholic beverages, spa treatments and tips. Cruises are a convenient and fun way to see exotic parts of the world, such as Mexico, the Greek Isles, Asia, or New Zealand and Australia.

All-inclusive resorts are another great option that takes most of the guesswork out of pricing and budgeting. For one price, everything, from the rooms to meals to alcohol, is included. Most packages also include things like spa treatments, rounds of golf, and daily excursions and tours. Many resorts will provide special extras for honeymooners, including in-room jacuzzis, champagne, roses, massages, luxury bath products and more. All-inclusive packages are found all over the world. You may want to consider one of the many all-inclusive resorts that cater to newlyweds or adults only, such as Sandals.

Another popular package is Disney's Fairy Tale Honeymoons. These include accommodations at Disney's exclusive resorts and admission to their theme parks.

Prices for Disney packages can range greatly depending on your tastes and the amount of activity you desire.

Finally, less traditional honeymoons that are growing in popularity include an African wildlife safari, camping, wine tasting in Italy, and eco-friendly trips in places like Costa Rica.

You and your fiancée should each make a wishlist to determine the type of weather, activities, accommodations and amenities you both imagine for your honeymoon. Put a star by the items you feel are most important, and this will give you a great place to start planning.

Next, you need to create a budget based on your wishlist. You want your honeymoon to be luxurious, romantic and offer priceless memories, but you also want to create a reasonable budget. Some couples find that creating a honeymoon registry is a great way for friends and family to contribute to the trip. The Dollar Dance is another tradition. The bride and groom dance with their guests while accepting the dollar "dance fee" as a contribution to the honeymoon. Whatever you choose, planning and sticking to a budget ensures that you'll have a memorable and beautiful honeymoon without spending a fortune.

The table in this chapter helps you create your honeymoon budget. If you find that you are going over your budget, review your wishlist and eliminate a few lower priority items to free up some money for the most important ones. If you find you are under budget, celebrate with a special "gift" for yourselves (massages, a nice dinner, etc.).

Enjoy planning the honeymoon getaway you've always dreamed of!

GENERAL BUDGET

Amount groom is able to contribute
from current funds/savings: $ _____

Amount bride is able to contribute
from current funds/savings: $ _____

Amount to be saved/acquired
by groom from now until the
honeymoon date (monthly
contributions, part-time job, gifts,
bonuses): $ _____

Amount to be saved/acquired
by bride from now until the
honeymoon date (monthly
contributions, part-time job, gifts,
bonuses): $ _____

Contributions from family, Dollar
Dance, honeymoon registry, etc.: $ _____

General Budget Total Amount: $ _____

BEFORE THE HONEYMOON

Special honeymoon clothing
purchases: $ _____

Bride's trousseau (honeymoon
lingerie): $ _____

Toiletries: $ _____

Camera, batteries, film, video
camera: $ _____

Guidebooks, travel magazines: $ _____

Foreign language books and CDs,
translation dictionary: $ _____

Passport photos, application fees for
international travel: $ _____

Medical exam, inoculations for
international travel: $ _____

**Before the Honeymoon Total
Amount:** $ _____

DURING THE HONEYMOON

TRANSPORTATION

Airplane tickets: $ _____

Shuttle or cab
(to and from the airport): $ _____

Car rental, gasoline, tolls: $ _____

Taxis, buses, other public
transportation: $ _____

Transportation Total Amount: $ _____

ACCOMMODATIONS

Hotel/resort room (total for entire
stay): $ _____

Room service: $ _____

Miscellaneous "hidden costs"
(Phone use, Internet, room taxes
and surcharges, chambermaid tips,
in-room liquor bar and snacks): $ _____

Accommodations Total Amount: $ _____

DURING THE HONEYMOON

MEALS

Breakfast:

$ _____ per meal x _____ # of days = $ _____

Lunch:

$ _____ per meal x _____ # of days = $ _____

Casual Dinners:

$ _____ per meal x _____ # of days = $ _____

Formal Dinners:

$ _____ per meal x _____ # of days = $ _____

Picnics, Snacks:

$ _____ per meal x _____ # of days = $ _____

Meals Total Amount: $ _____

DETAILED BUDGET DURING THE HONEYMOON

ENTERTAINMENT

Sport and activity lessons (tennis,
golf, ballroom dancing, etc.): $ _____

Day excursions and tours (boat
tours, diving, snorkeling, bus and
guided tours, etc.): $ _____

Shows, theatre, concerts: $ _____

Lounges, nightclubs, discos (don't
forget to include the cost of drinks
and bar gratuities): $ _____

Museum fees: $ _____

Pampering (massages, spa
treatments, nail salon, etc.): $ _____

Gambling: $ _____

Theme parks: $ _____

Entertainment Total Amount: $ _____

DETAILED BUDGET DURING THE HONEYMOON

MISCELLANEOUS

Shopping: $ _____

Souvenirs for yourselves: $ _____

Souvenirs and gifts for family and
friends: $ _____

Postcards (including cost of stamps): $ _____

Newspapers and magazines: $ _____

Replacement toiletries, medicines,
other: $ _____

Miscellaneous Total Amount: $ _____

AFTER THE HONEYMOON

Photo printing, online photo storage
space: $ _____

Photo albums: $ _____

**After the Honeymoon Total
Amount:** $ _____

INTERNATIONAL HONEYMOON TRAVEL GUIDELINES

If you are traveling abroad for your honeymoon, you will need extra assistance to determine the requirements and recommendations for your chosen travel destination.

There are over 250 U.S. embassies and consulates around the world. After contacting the Tourism Bureau for the area you will be traveling to, it is also a wise idea to contact the U.S. Embassy or Consulate for that region. Within this section you will find numerous resources to assure all of your questions and concerns are addressed before you travel.

PASSPORTS AND VISAS

As a U.S. citizen, you need a passport book to enter and to depart most foreign countries and to reenter the United States. Passport books can be obtained from one of the 13 U.S. Passport Agencies or one of the thousands of authorized passport locations, such as state and federal courts, as well as some U.S. Post Offices. The current cost of a first-time passport is $110, plus a $25 processing fee. A passport renewal is $110, with no processing fee. If you are traveling abroad within 10 weeks of applying for a passport, you will need to have your application expedited, which is an additional $60 on top of the regular cost.

If you do not have a passport and are traveling to Canada, Mexico, the Caribbean, and Bermuda by land or sea only, you can apply for a passport card. A passport card is a wallet-size travel document that provides a less expensive, smaller, and convenient alternative to the passport book. Note that a passport card is not valid for air travel.

You should always check to see what the country you're honeymooning in requires, and do so several months in advance to allow time to renew or apply for passports. Keep in mind that January through July is a busier time and the process may take longer.

Some countries also require visas. A visa is an endorsement by officials of a foreign country as permission to visit their country. You first need a passport in order to obtain a visa. Inquire with the resources listed in this section for requirements of your specific destination.

Note that the bride should have her passport and airline tickets reflect her maiden name for ease in proof of identification while traveling. Name changes can be processed after returning from the honeymoon with your marriage certificate.

Your passport will be one of the most important documents you will take on your honeymoon. Contact the local U.S. Embassy immediately if your passport becomes lost or stolen. Have a photocopy of your passport's data page, date and place of issuance, and passport number to be kept with a contact person at home. You should also travel with a set of these photocopies in addition to an extra set of passport photos for speed in attaining a replacement.

In addition to calling the U.S. Passport Agencies for personal assistance, you can also call their 24-hour recorded information lines for information on agency locations, travel advisories and warnings, and Consular Information Sheets pertaining to every country in the world.

Additional, official information for U.S. citizens regarding international travel can be found at http://travel.state.gov.

Foreign embassies and consulates located in the U.S. can provide current information regarding their country.

UNITED STATES PASSPORT AGENCIES

Boston Passport Agency
Thomas P. O'Neil Federal Building
Room 247, 10 Causeway Street
Boston, Massachusetts 02222-1094

Chicago Passport Agency
Kluczynski Federal Building
Suite 380, 230 South Dearborn Street
Chicago, Illinois 60604-1564

Honolulu Passport Agency
First Hawaii Tower
1132 Bishop St., Suite 500
Honolulu, Hawaii 96813-2809

Houston Passport Agency
Mickey Leland Federal Building
1919 Smith Street, Suite 1100
Houston, Texas 77002-8049

Los Angeles Passport Agency
11000 Wilshire Blvd., Room 13100
Los Angeles, California 90024-3615

Miami Passport Agency
Claude Pepper Federal Office Building, 3rd Floor
51 Southwest First Avenue
Miami, Florida 33130-1680

New Orleans Passport Agency
Postal Services Building, Room T-12005
701 Loyola Avenue
New Orleans, Louisiana 70113-1931

New York Passport Agency
Rockefeller Center, Room 270
630 Fifth Avenue
New York, New York 10111-0031

Philadelphia Passport Agency
U.S. Customs House
200 Chestnut Street Room 103
Philadelphia, Pennsylvania 19106-2970

San Francisco Passport Agency
555 Montgomery
San Francisco, California 94101

Seattle Passport Agency
Federal Office Building, Room 992
915 Second Avenue
Seattle, Washington 98174-1091

Stamford Passport Agency
One Landmark Square
Broad and Atlantic Streets
Stamford, Connecticut 06901-2667

Washington Passport Agency
1111 19th Street, N.W.
Washington, D.C. 20522-1705

HEALTH CONCERNS

In the United States, the National Center for Infectious Diseases (NCID) and the Centers for Disease Control and Prevention (CDC) provide the most current information pertinent to international travel. The World Health Organization (WHO) concerns itself with general and specific health issues for almost every part of the world. Health and safety issues as related to international travel are the basis for the International Heath Regulations adopted by the World Health Organization.

Your travel agent should be fully informed about current conditions and requirements. Your personal physician should also be able to provide you with information and advice for traveling in the region you visit.

TRAVELERS' HEALTH INSURANCE COVERAGE

If your health insurance policy does not cover you abroad, consider acquiring a temporary health insurance policy. In addition to health insurance coverage, many policy packages include protection in case of trip cancellation and baggage loss.

PRESCRIPTION MEDICATIONS

Keep prescription medications in their original pharmacy containers with the original labels. Bring a copy of your prescriptions and note the drug's generic name. You may consider getting a letter from your physician warranting your need for the medication.